Contents

Why Teach Handwriting?

Despite the influx of technological communication instruments that require only voice and/or button-pushing in today's world, handwriting is still an important life skill. Writing by hand ties in closely with the skills of reading and comprehending. Handwriting personalizes communication with others in a way that technological devices cannot. Neat, legible printing leads to neat, legible cursive writing. Handwriting is a skill that students can take pride in throughout their lives.

Teacher Tips

When preparing to teach printing to young students, consider materials to have available, your method of teaching, how to motivate students, general support, and ways to monitor and assess students' progress. Here are tips and suggestions for each of these aspects.

Materials to Have Available

A printing centre is an excellent way to give students a variety of opportunities to practise their letter formation with a variety of materials. You may wish to include the following:

- practice printing sheets
- whiteboards
- laminated printing practice cards and lined paper
- chalkboards
- individual notebooks, portfolios, or scrapbooks
- centre cards with simple phrases, poems, etc., to copy
- pencil grips
- different sizes and colours of paper
- pencils, coloured pencils, markers, and crayons

Methods of Teaching

- Teach the formation of letters in small groups of Modelled Printing sessions.
- Focus on one letter at a time, especially for students just starting to learn how to print. Use lined chart paper or wide lines on a whiteboard or chalkboard to model printing.
- Teach letters with a similar formation in clusters. For example,

  - E, F, H, I, L, and T
  - V, W, and X
  - K, M, N, and Y
  - A and Z
  - C and O
  - G, Q, and S
  - B, D, J, P, R, and U

- While introducing a letter, model the formation of the letter, describing out loud the direction of the strokes used to form the letter.
- Repeat the directions for forming the letter while students imitate making the letter in the air with big arm movements. Also have students form the letters with their eyes closed.
- Invite students to print the letter on the chart paper or board. Encourage them to describe their movements out loud, as you previously modelled.
- Consider teaching both upper-case and lower-case forms of the same letter at the same time, especially if you are tying the printing lesson in with letter recognition and possibly phonetics.
- Use the practice sheets found in this resource as immediate follow-up to each lesson. Have students circle their best letter on each line as a form of self-assessment.
- Make sure to reinforce good posture habits while students practise their writing skills. Slouching will create unnecessary strain on students' young spines.

Motivation for Students

Consider these ideas for motivating students to practise their printing skills, see progress, feel pride in accomplishment, and have a product to show for their hard work:

- Keep students' work organized in a portfolio, folder, or scrapbook, or bind practice pages into a book for each student.
- As students complete printing lessons successfully, have them color in their personal completion chart provided in this resource.
- For proficient printers, provide short poems and nursery rhymes to copy. Encourage students to illustrate their pages, then to bind the pages together to make a book.

Other General Support

The classroom environment, and your attention to individual needs, can promote the learning of good handwriting. Here are tips and suggestions for helping students learn to print legibly:

• Model legible printing at every opportunity.

• Show students how to hold their writing tools properly (i.e., between the thumb and first finger, and resting on their middle finger).

• Consider providing "fat" pencils for beginners, or pencil grips as necessary.

• Ensure that pencils are sharpened before use.

• If you notice some students having difficulty with specific letters, call them together for small-group or individual instruction and review.

Encouraging Fine Motor Control and Finger Muscle Strength

Provide activities that increase fine motor control and finger muscle strength, such as:

• modelling clay to roll small balls, or to create sculptures with details

• art projects that involve using crayons, finger paints, scissors, or tearing paper

• building blocks that snap together

• paper clips to string together

• puzzles

• lacing or stitching cards

• paper to cut, paste, and fold

Support for Left-handed Students

Left-handed students often have difficulty forming some letters smoothly. Help them to be comfortable with their efforts.

• Be accepting if students make some strokes right to left, rather than left to right.

• Orient students' paper on a slight angle to the left. Students can shift the paper to the left as their writing progresses across the page.

• Encourage students to keep their left wrist straight, rather than hooked. (Hooking the wrist is a habit many left-handed writers develop so they can see what they have written.)

Monitoring Progress

• Use the rubrics and checklists in this resource to assess students' learning. Encourage students to self-assess their printing according to the rubric provided.

Pre-printing Practice

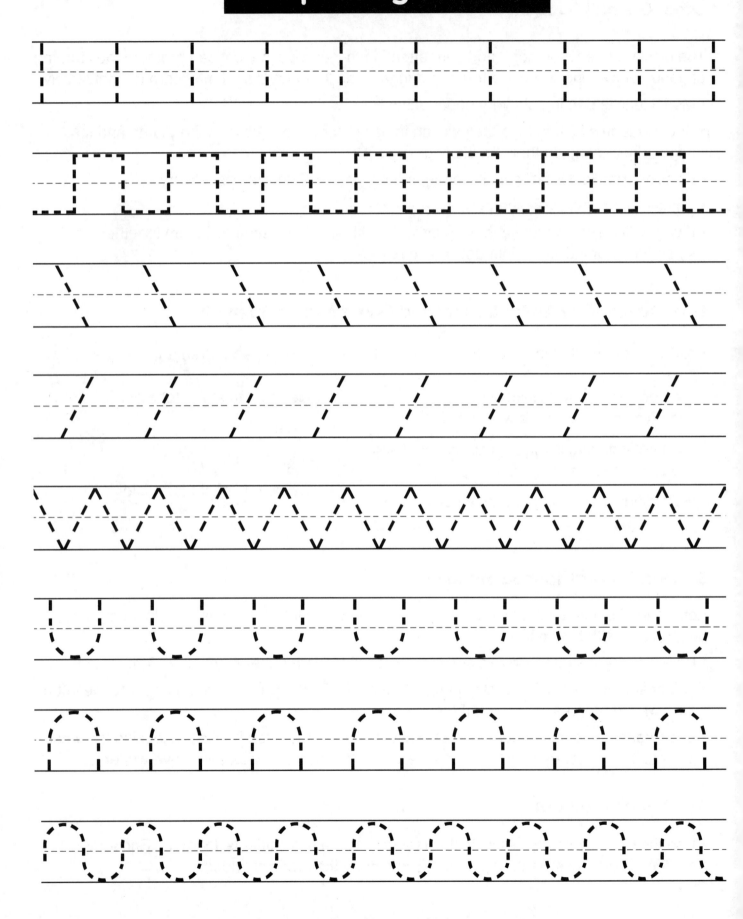

Printing Practice – Letters

Trace the following lower-case letters.

Trace the following upper-case letters.

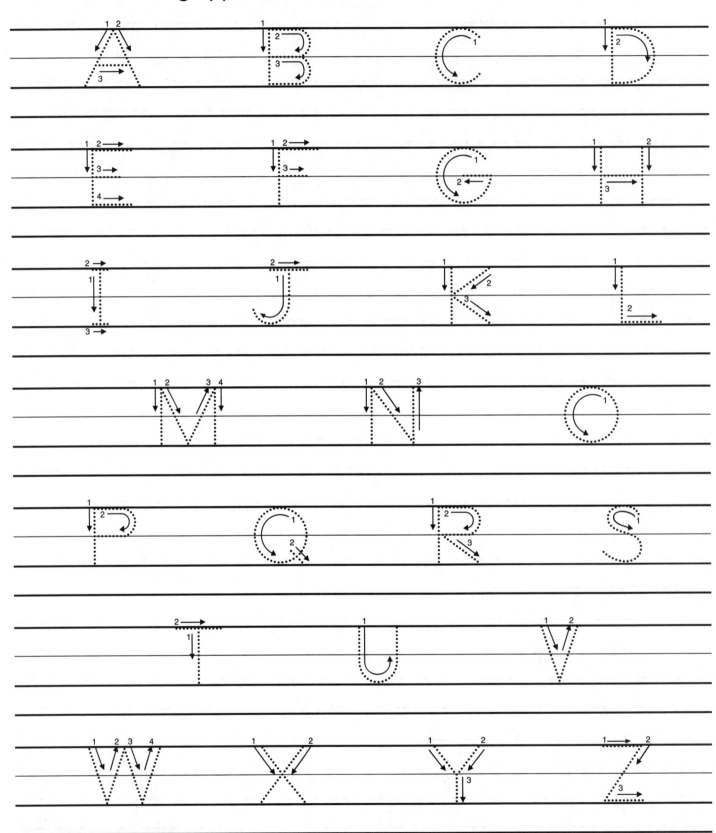

© Chalkboard Publishing

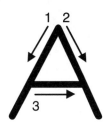

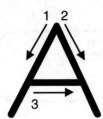

A A A A A A A

A

a a a a a a a

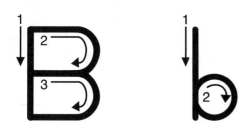

Trace and print. Circle your best B or b on each line.

B B B B B B B

b b b b b b b

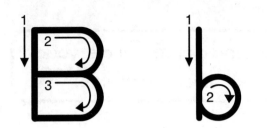

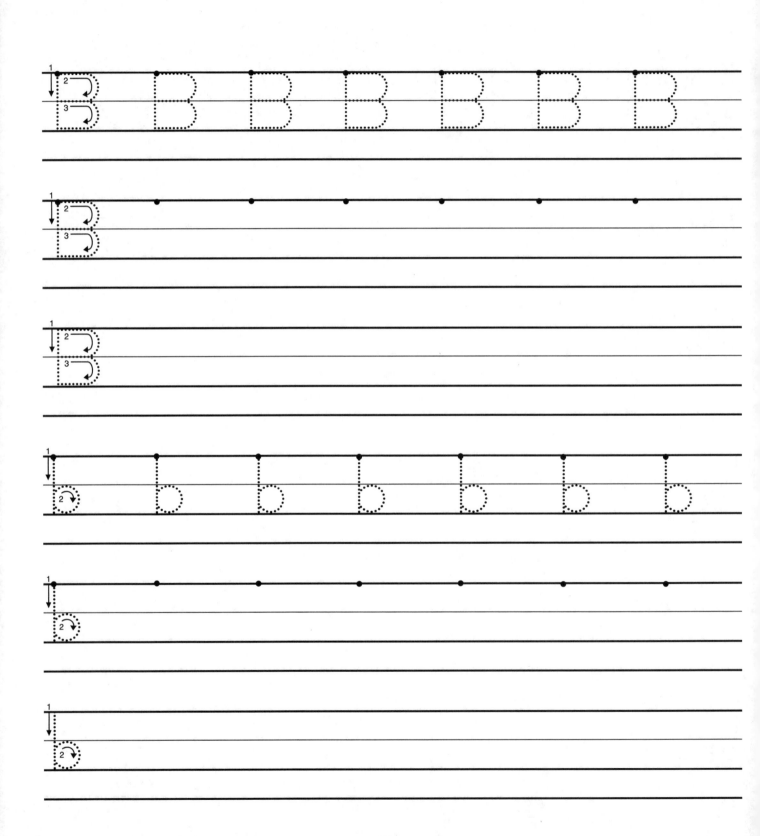

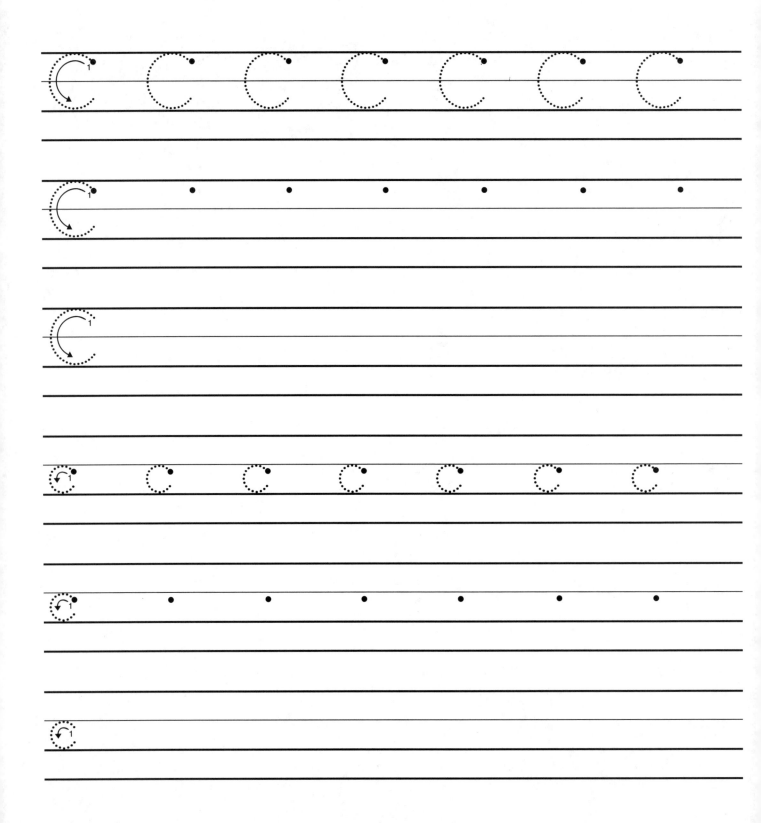

© Chalkboard Publishing

Trace and print. Circle your best D or d on each line.

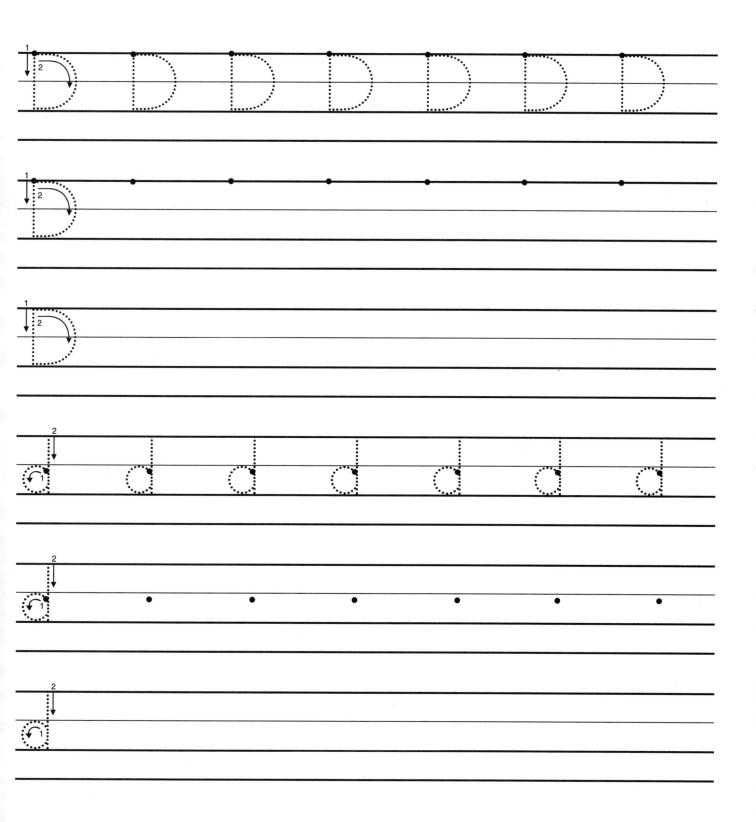

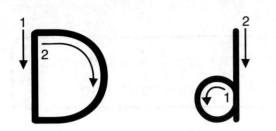

Trace and print. Circle your best D or d on each line.

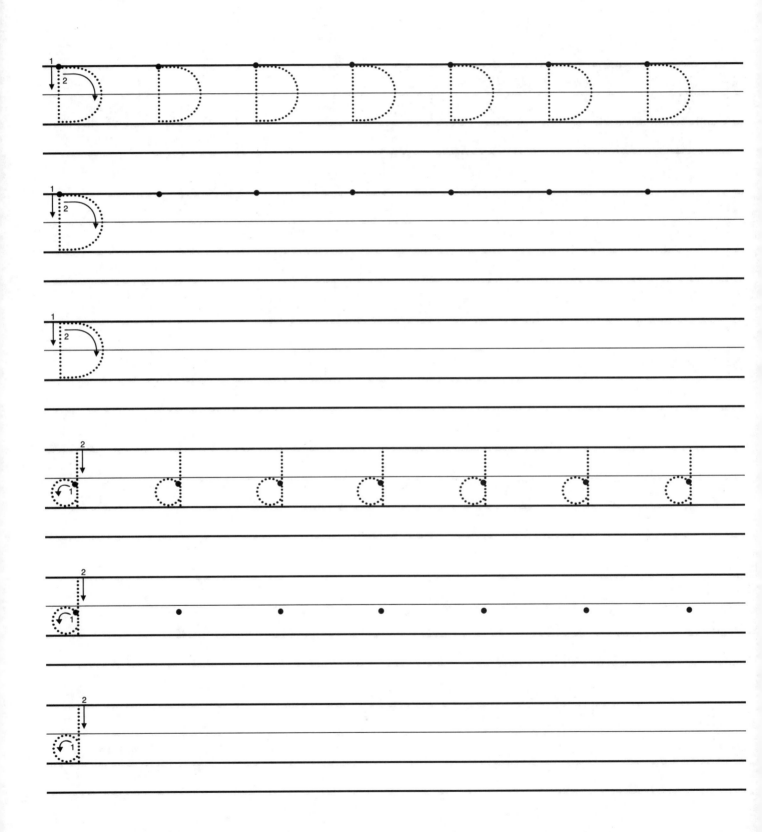

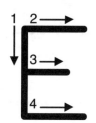

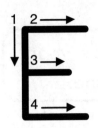

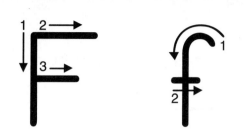

Trace and print. Circle your best F or f on each line.

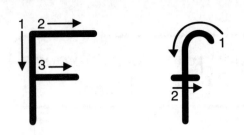

Trace and print. Circle your best F or f on each line.

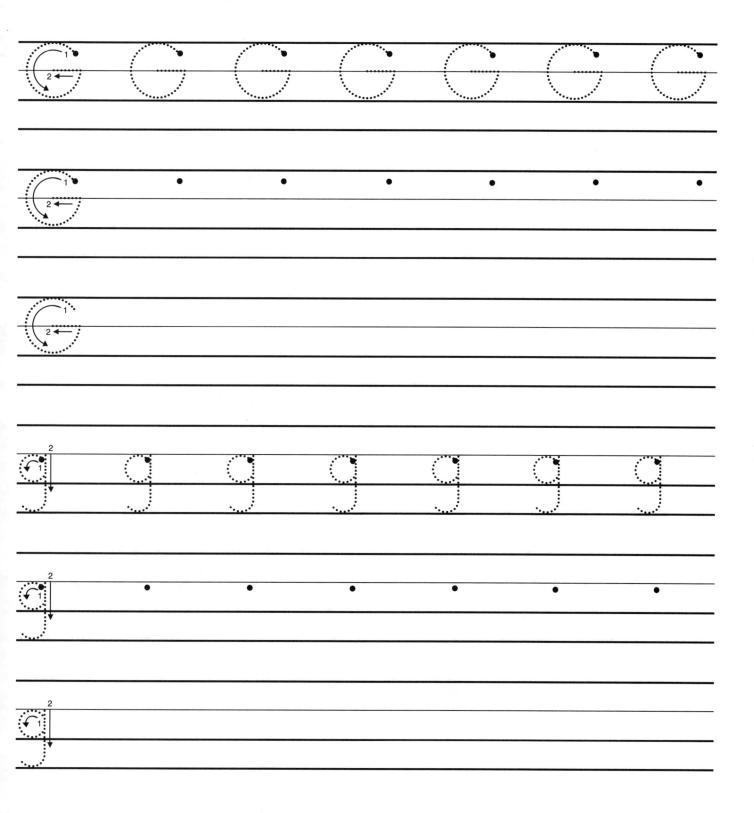

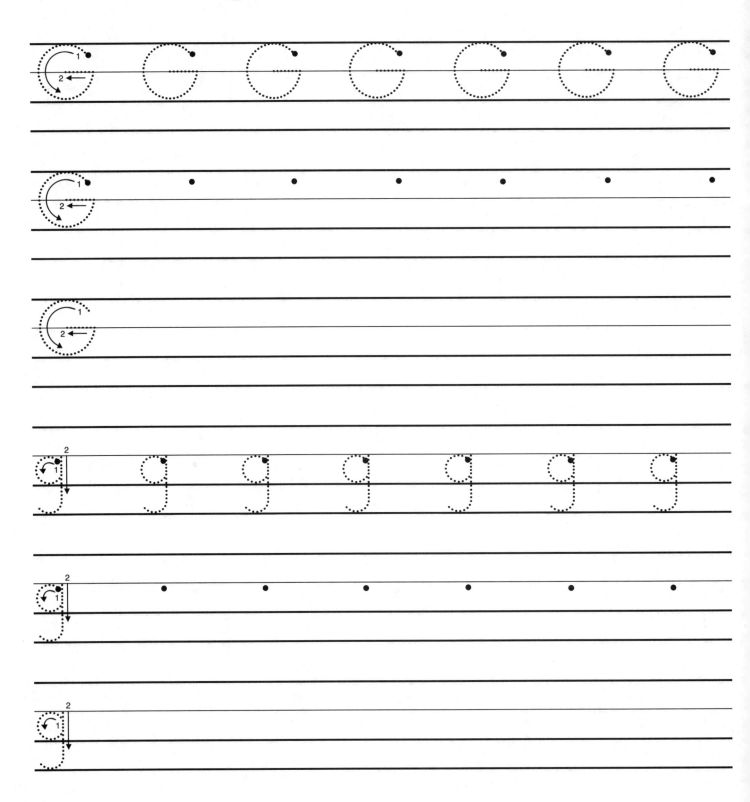

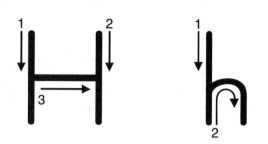

Trace and print. Circle your best H or h on each line.

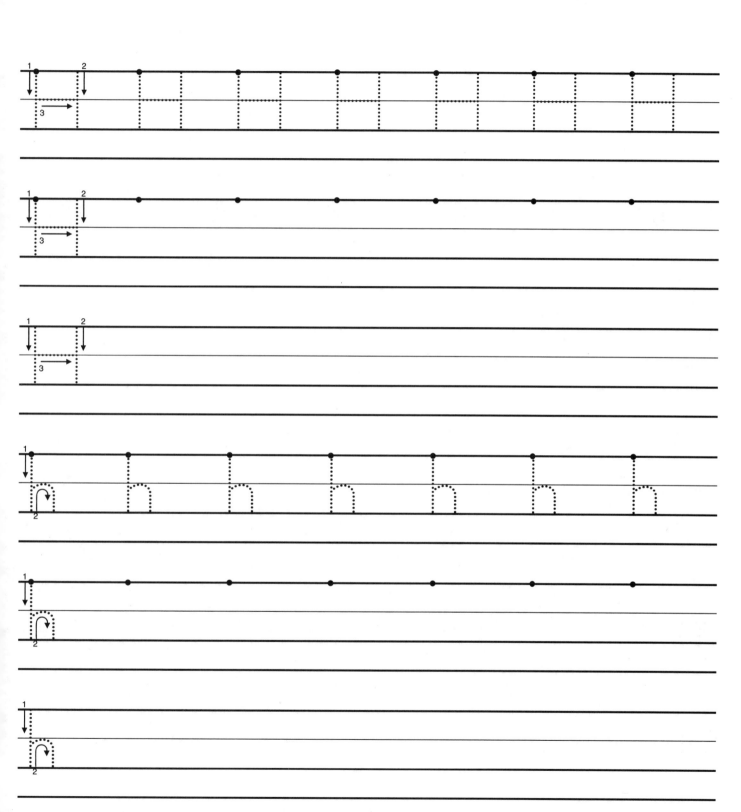

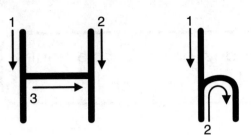

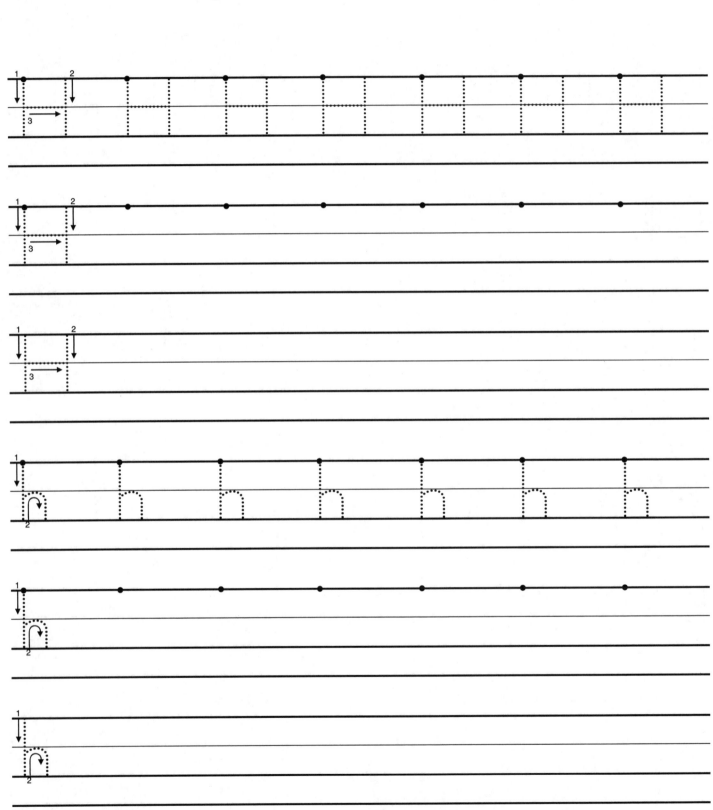

© Chalkboard Publishing

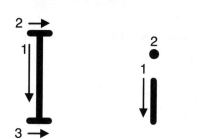

Trace and print. Circle your best I or i on each line.

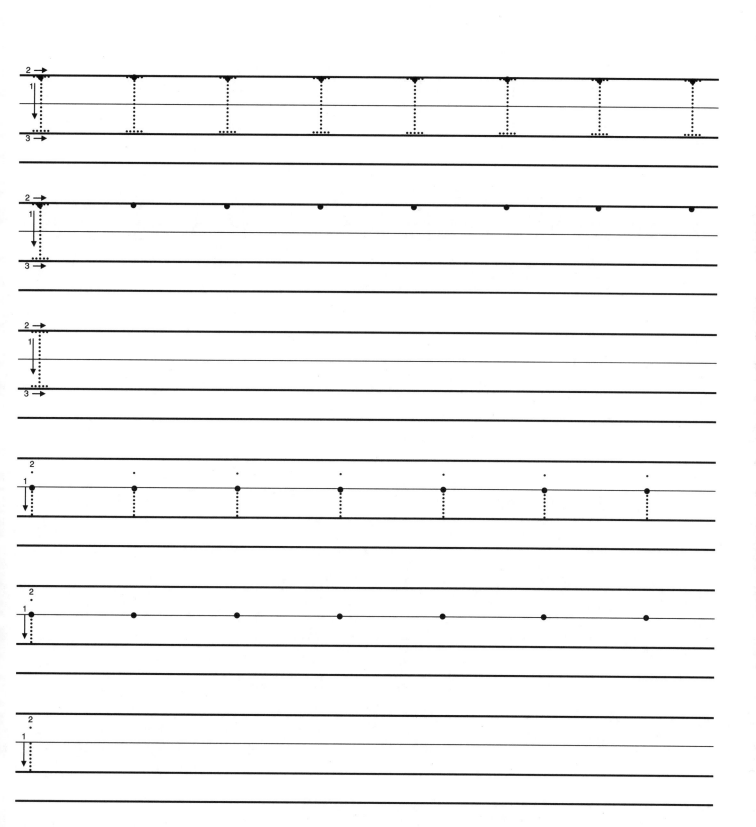

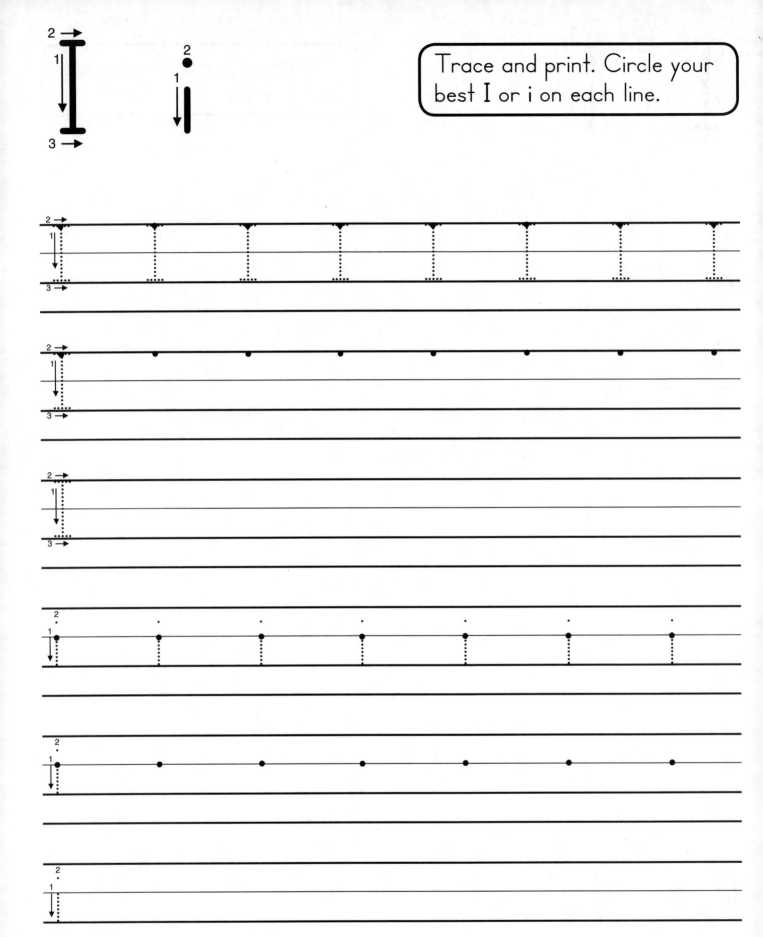

Trace and print. Circle your best I or i on each line.

© Chalkboard Publishing

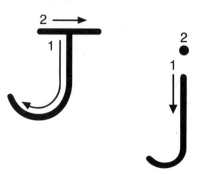

Trace and print. Circle your best J or j on each line.

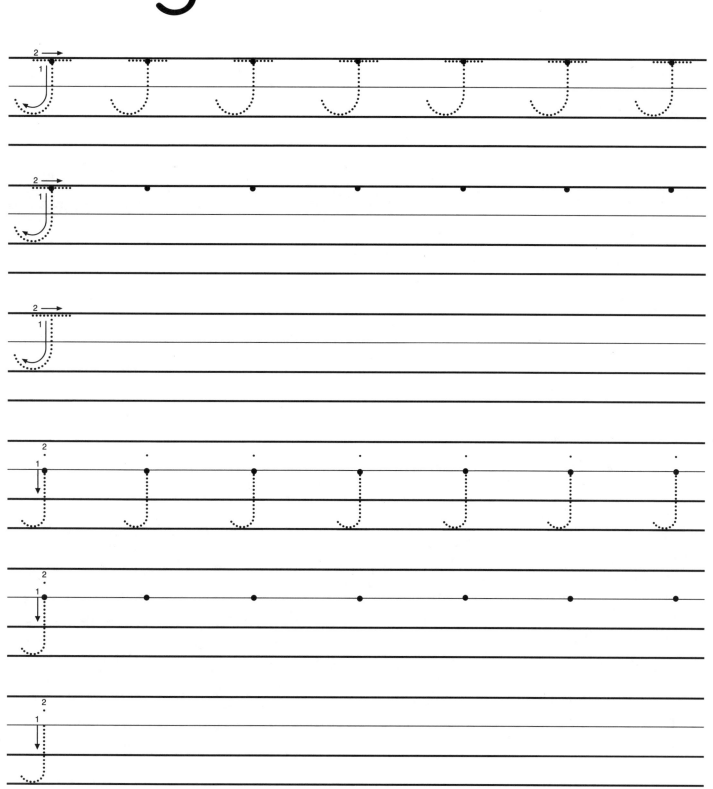

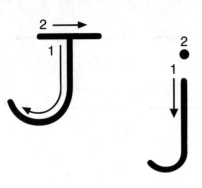

Trace and print. Circle your best J or j on each line.

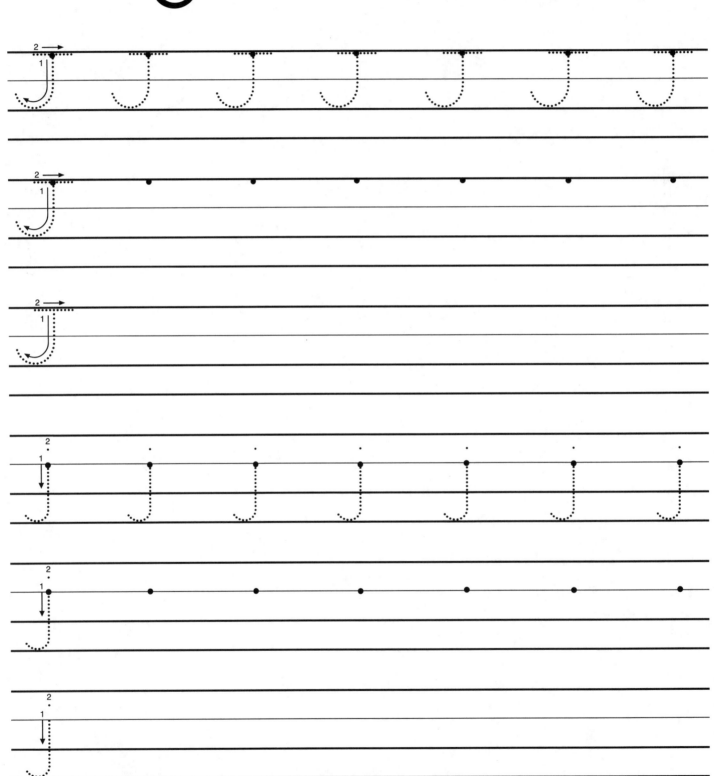

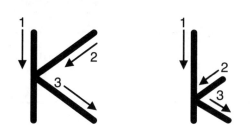

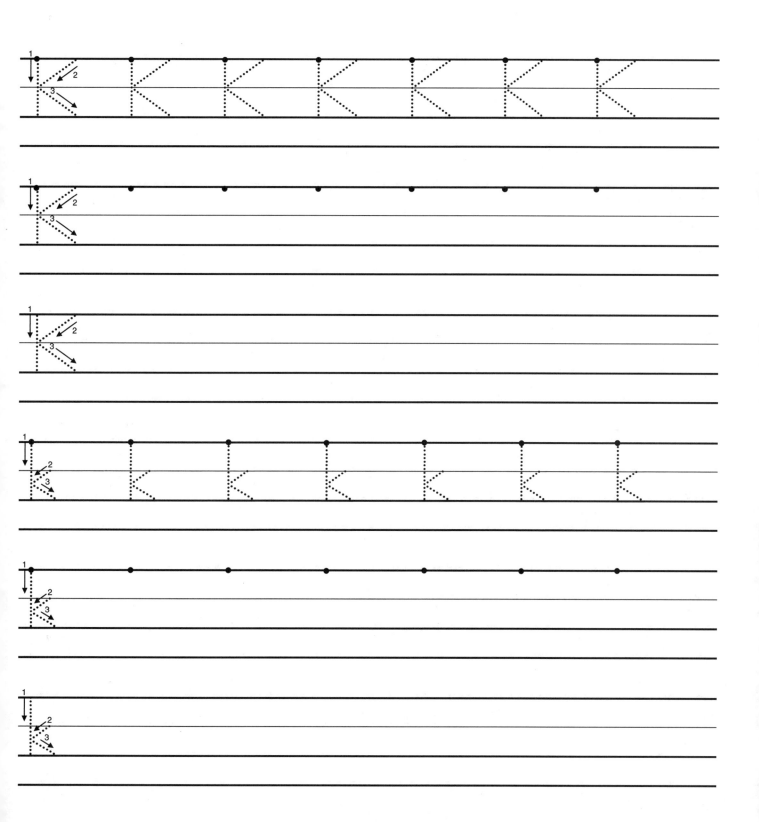

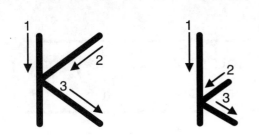

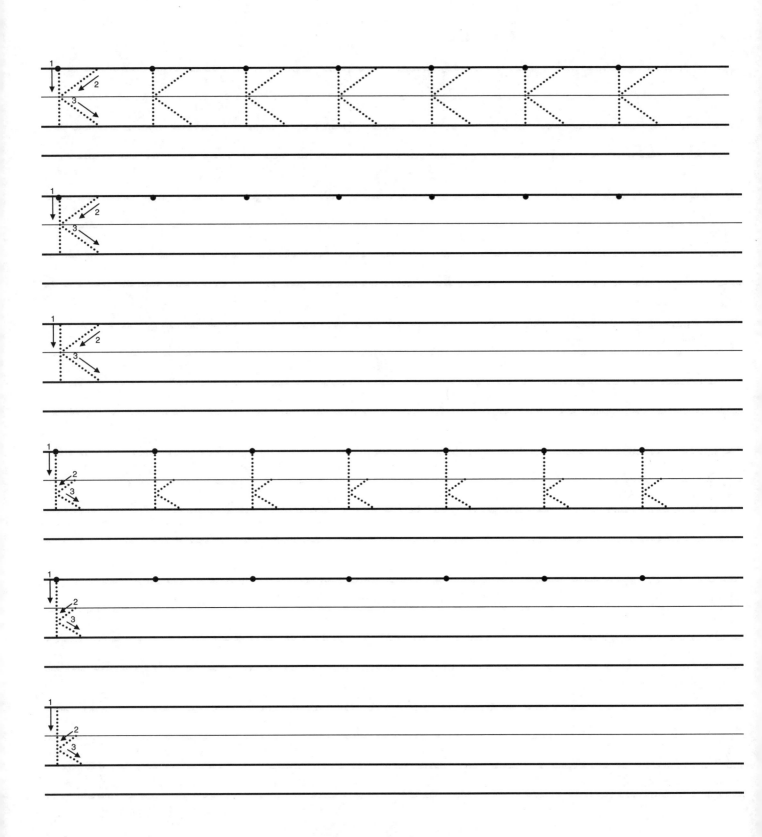

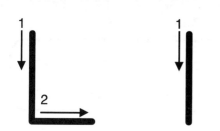

Trace and print. Circle your best L or I on each line.

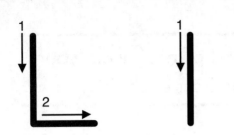

Trace and print. Circle your best L or l on each line.

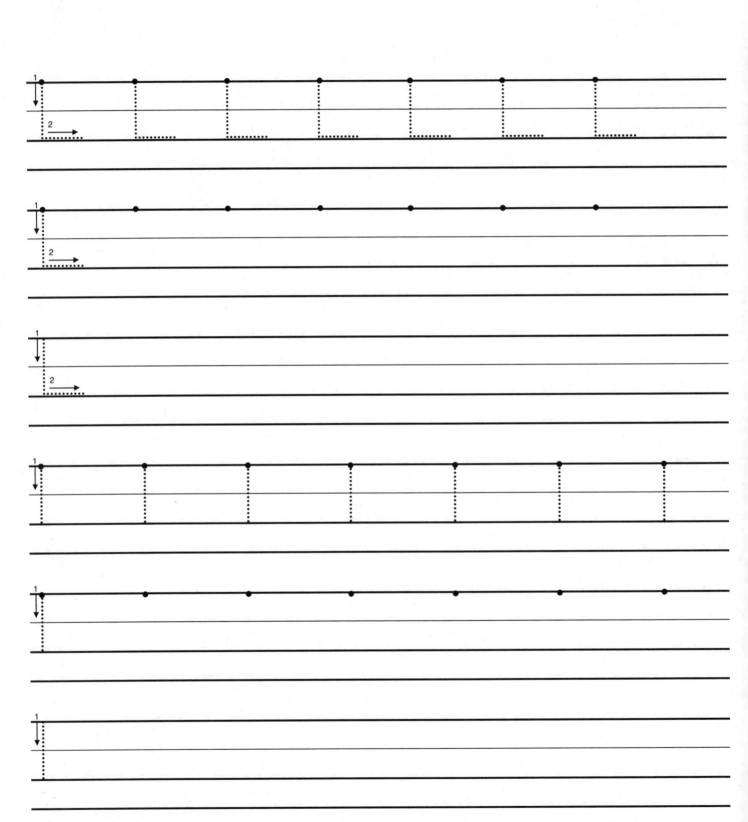

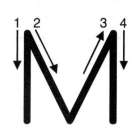

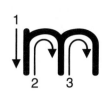

Trace and print. Circle your best M or m on each line.

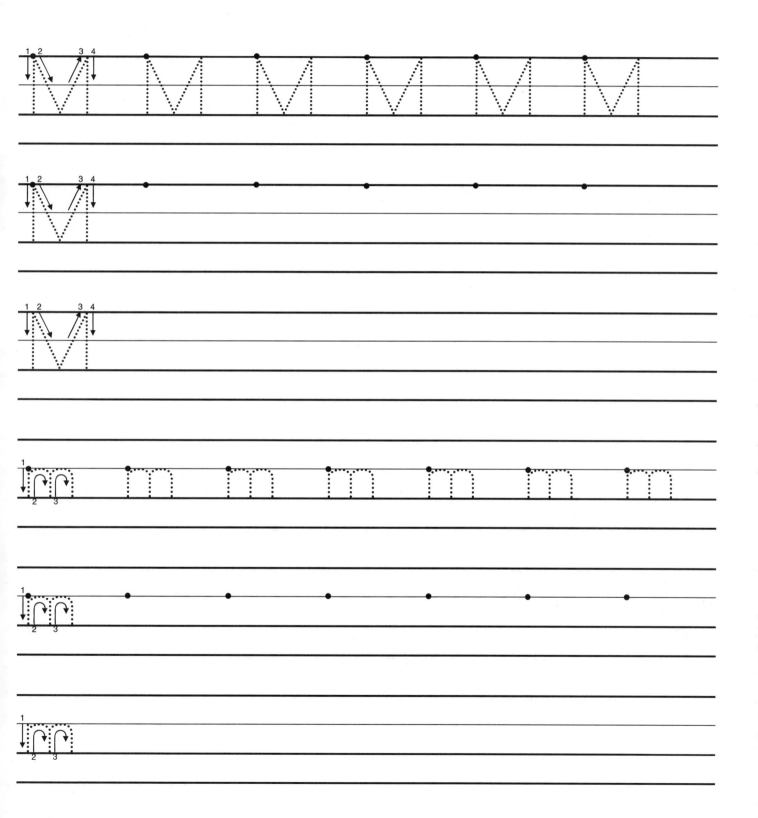

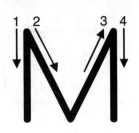

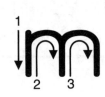

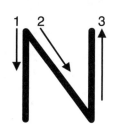

Trace and print. Circle your best N or n on each line.

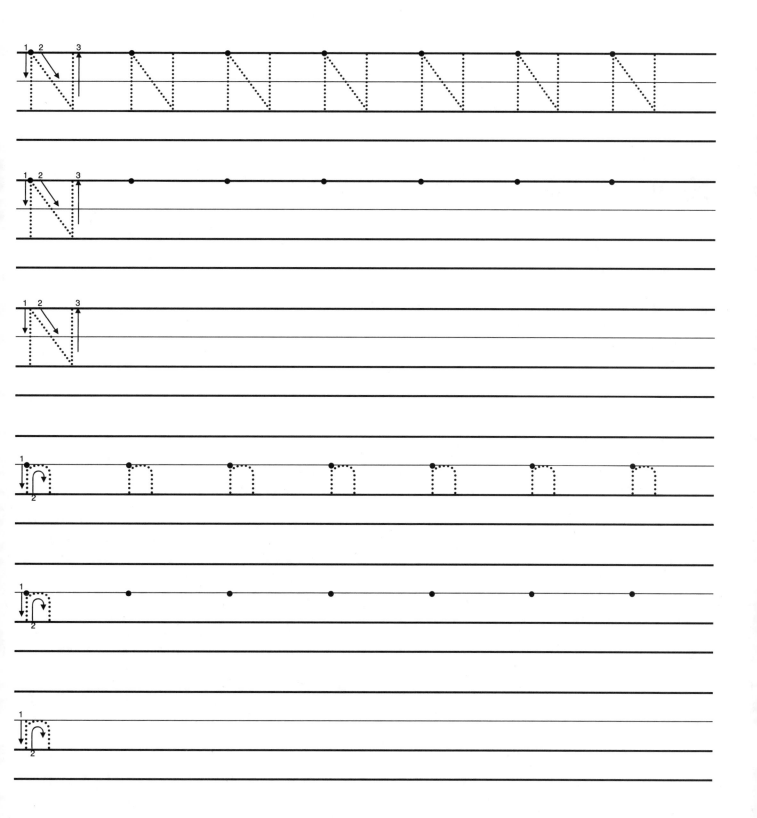

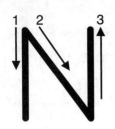

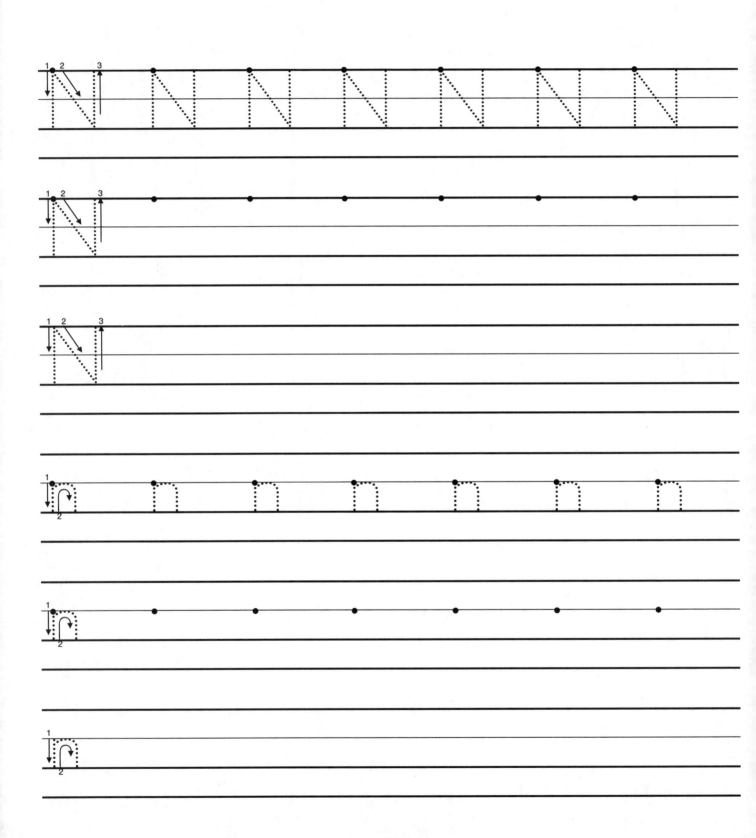

© Chalkboard Publishing

© Chalkboard Publishing

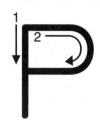 

Trace and print. Circle your best P or p on each line.

© Chalkboard Publishing

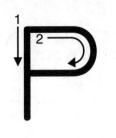 

Trace and print. Circle your best P or p on each line.

© Chalkboard Publishing

Trace and print. Circle your best Q or q on each line.

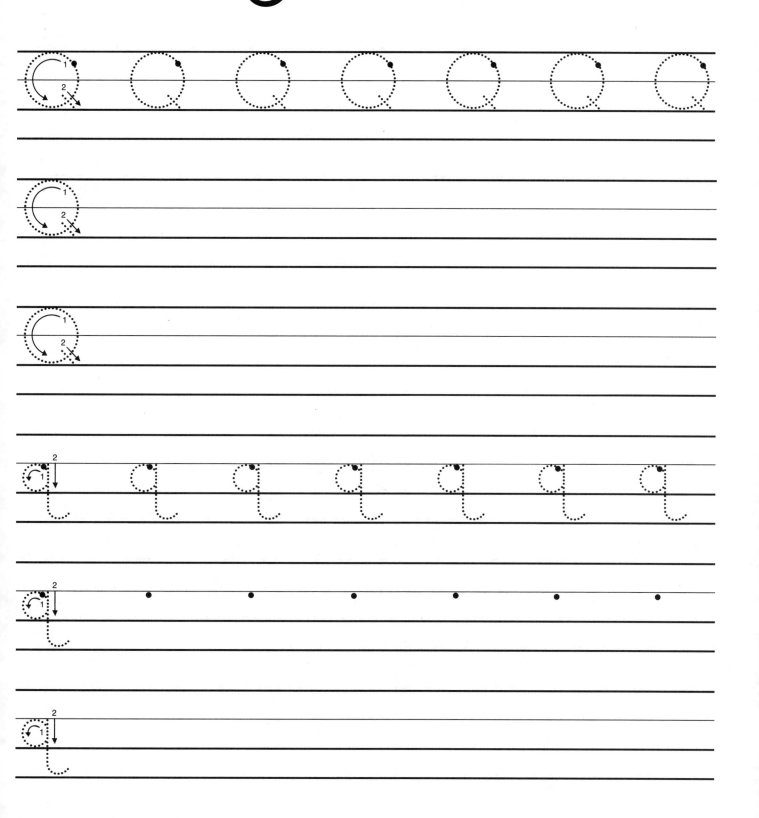

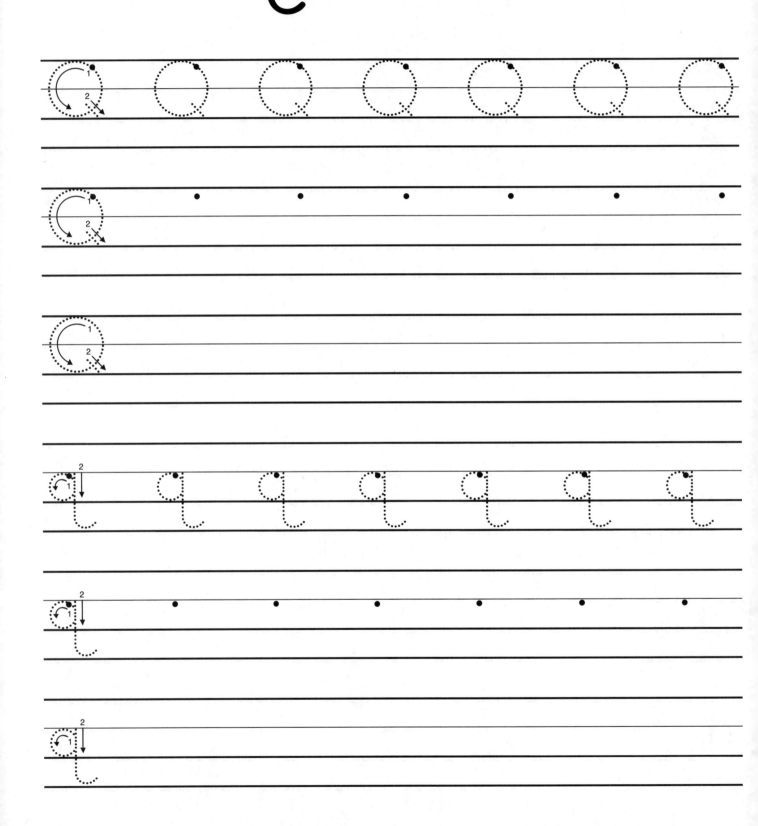

© Chalkboard Publishing

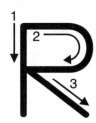

Trace and print. Circle your best R or r on each line.

© Chalkboard Publishing

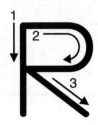

R R R R R R R

R

R

r r r r r r r

r

r

S S S S S S S

S

S

S S S S S S S

S

S

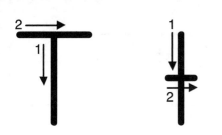

Trace and print. Circle your best T or t on each line.

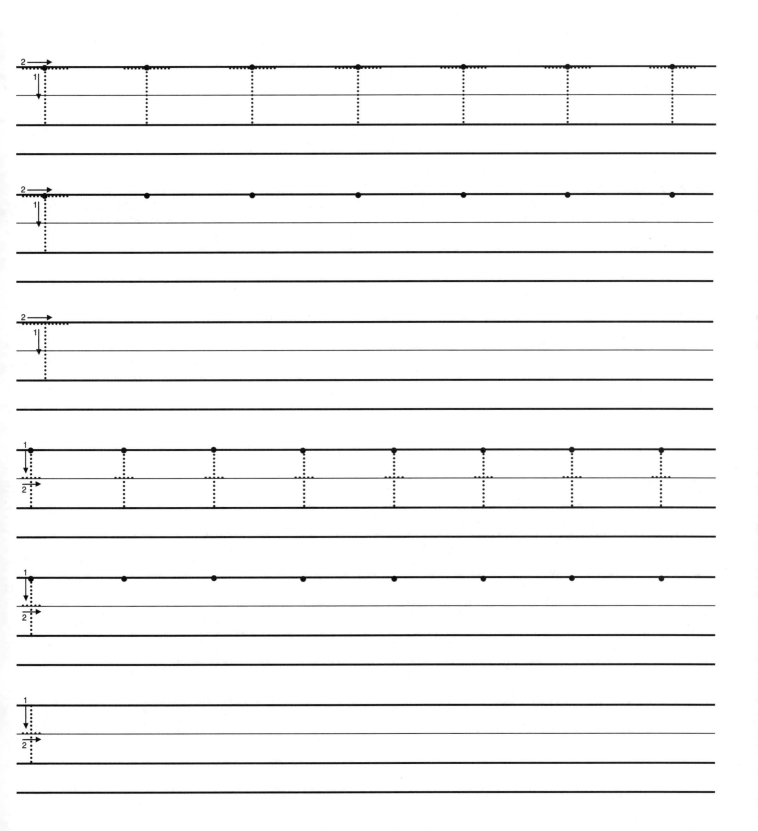

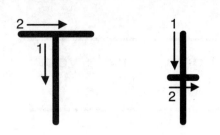

Trace and print. Circle your best T or t on each line.

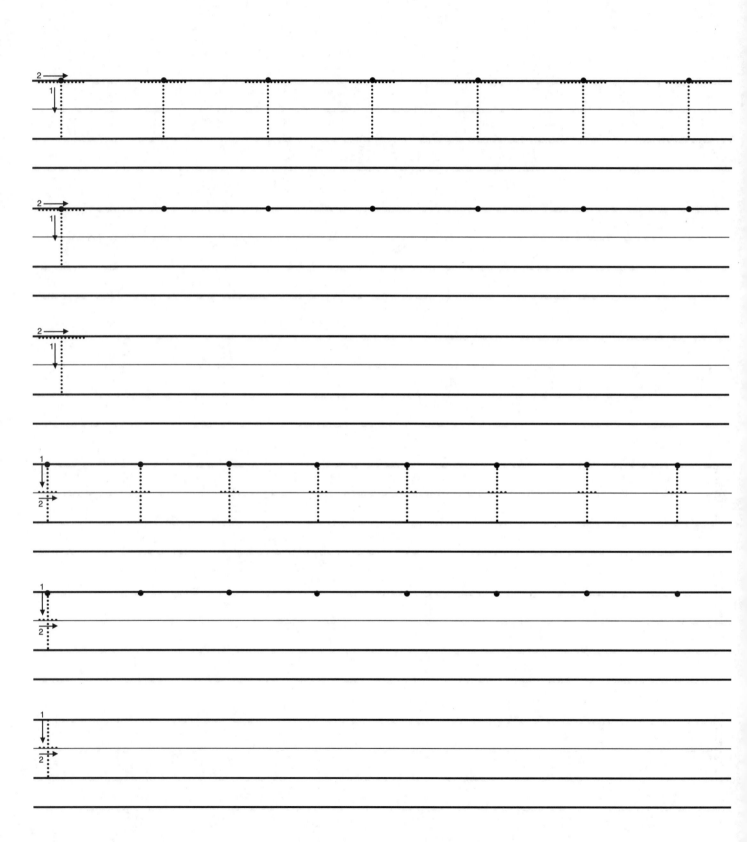

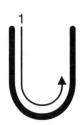

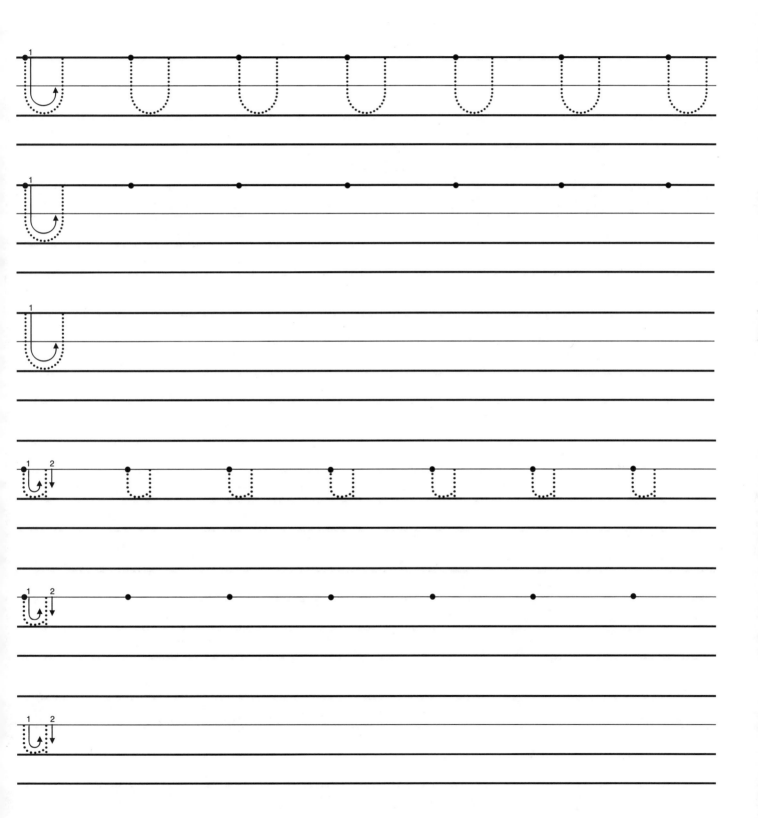

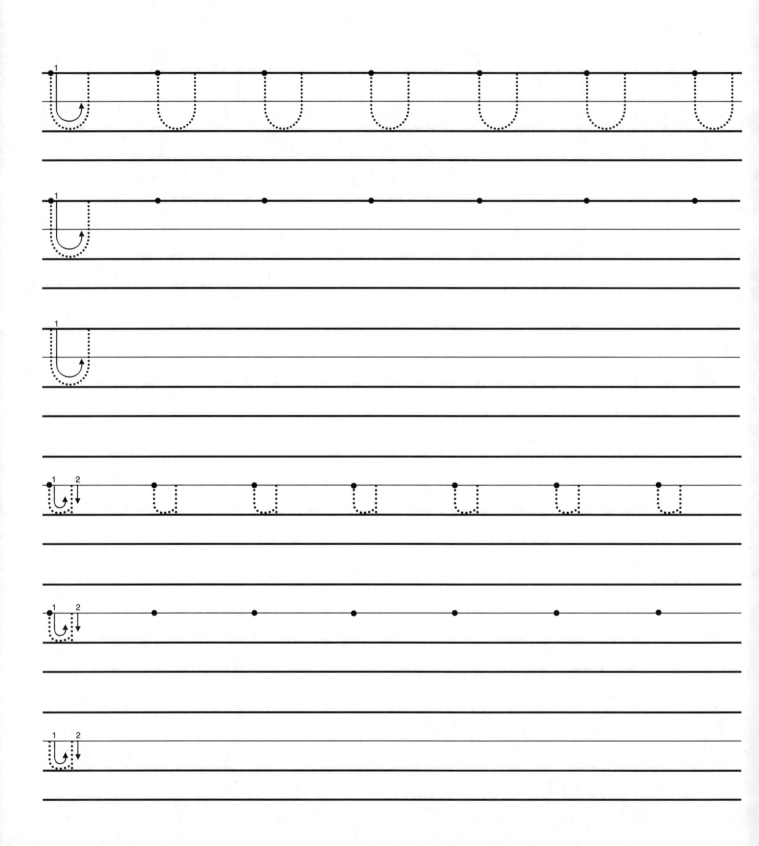

Trace and print. Circle your best V or v on each line.

V V V V V V V

V

V

v v v v v v v

v

v

V V V V V V V

V

V

v v v v v v v

v

v

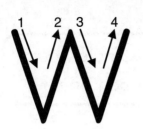

Trace and print. Circle your best W or w on each line.

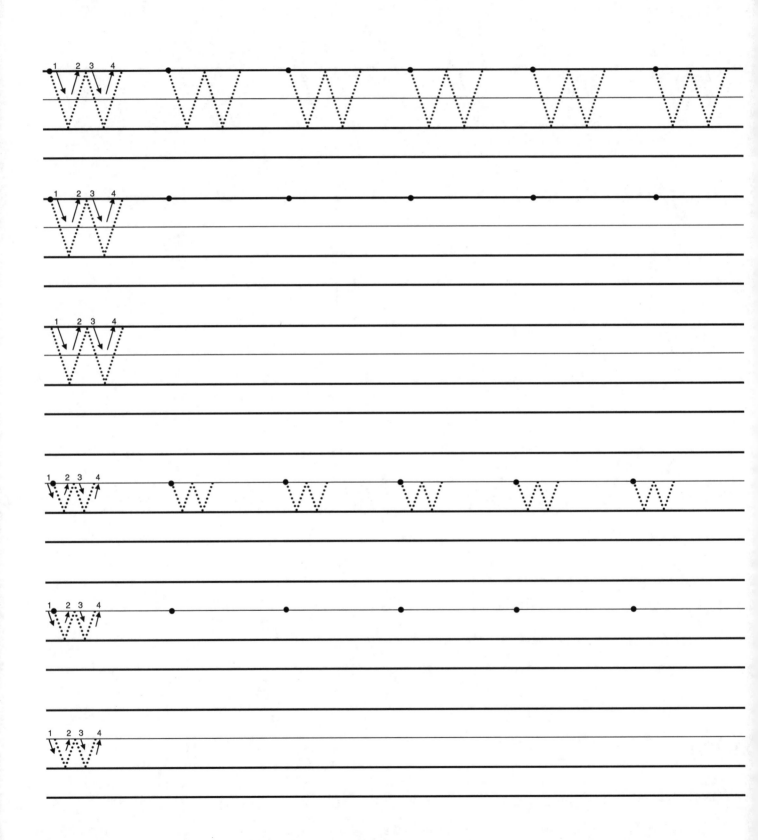

Trace and print. Circle your best X or x on each line.

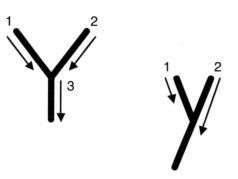

Trace and print. Circle your best Y or y on each line.

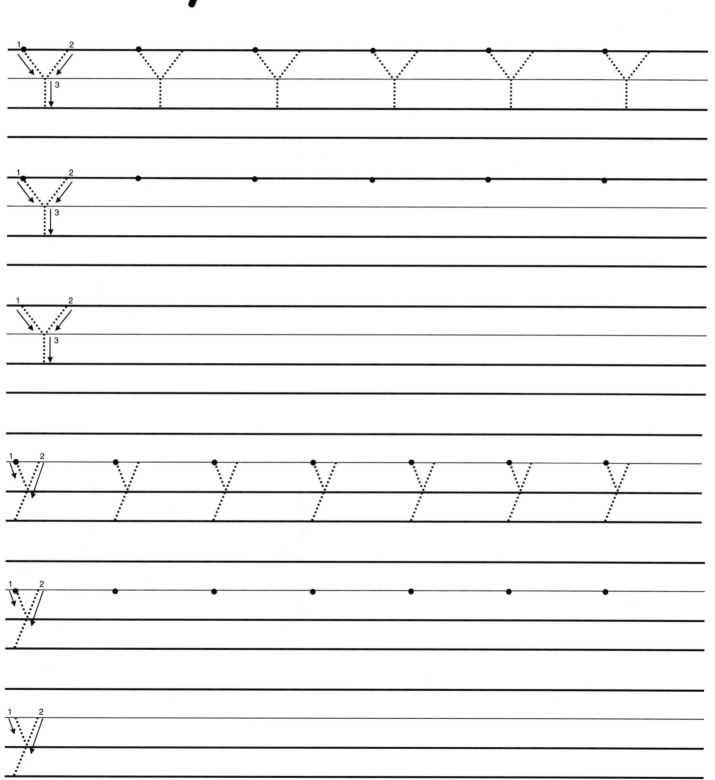

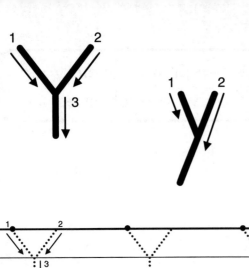

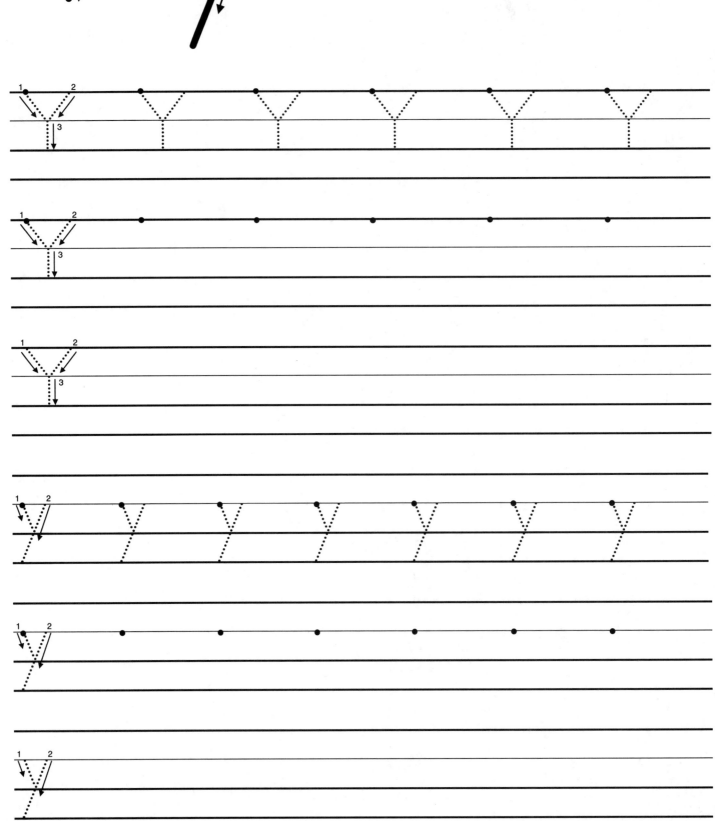

Trace and print. Circle your best Z or z on each line.

© Chalkboard Publishing

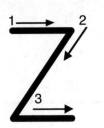

© Chalkboard Publishing

A a

airplane

What other words start with the letter a?

a   a

a   a

B b

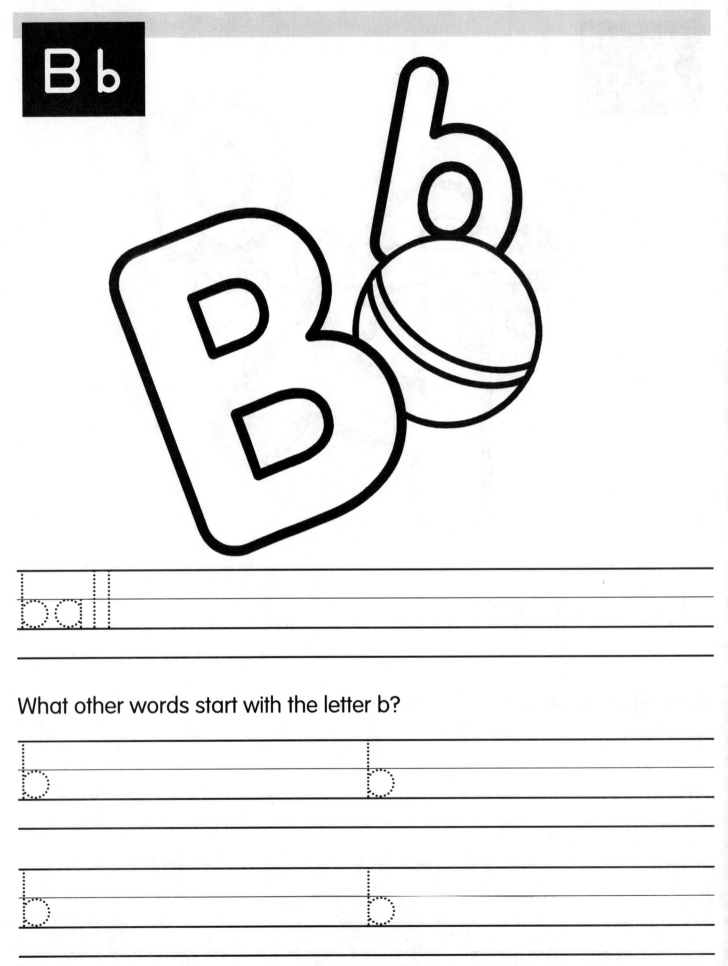

b̶a̶l̶l̶

What other words start with the letter b?

b̶

b̶

b̶

b̶

C c

clock

What other words start with the letter c?

c   c

c   c

D d

drum

What other words start with the letter d?

d   d

d   d

E e

earth

What other words start with the letter e?

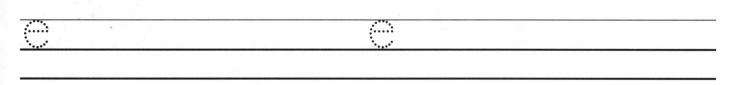

e   e

e   e

F f

fish

What other words start with the letter f?

f   f

f   f

G g

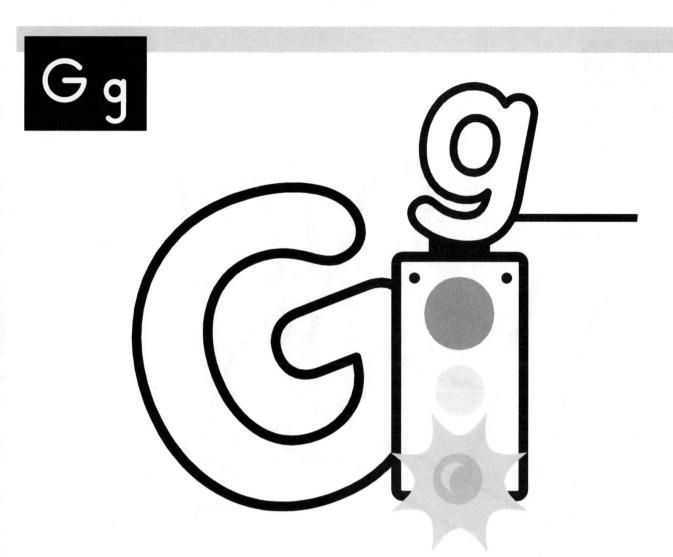

green

What other words start with the letter g?

g .... g

g .... g

H h

hammer

What other words start with the letter h?

h   h

h   h

I i

ice cream

What other words start with the letter i?

J j

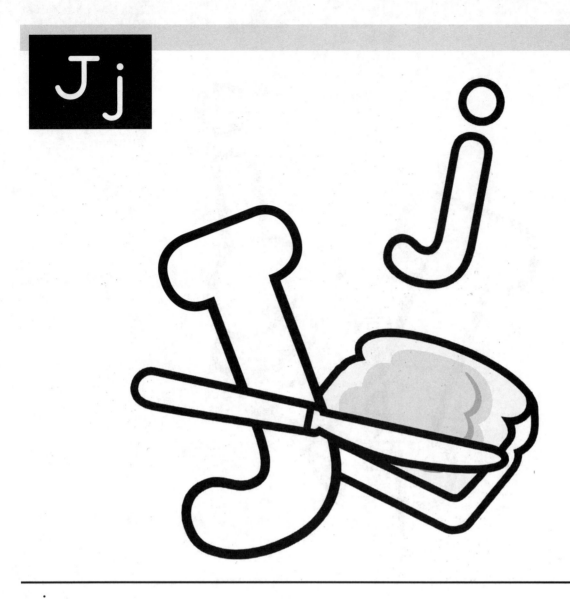

jam

What other words start with the letter j?

K k

kite

What other words start with the letter k?

k   k

k   k

L l

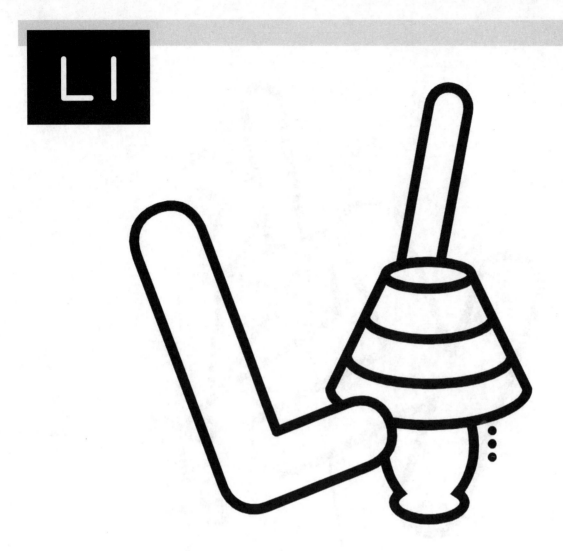

lamp

What other words start with the letter l?

© Chalkboard Publishing

M m

magic

What other words start with the letter m?

m   m

m   m

N n

nest

What other words start with the letter n?

n　　　　　　n

n　　　　　　n

Oo

octopus

What other words start with the letter o?

o

o

o

o

P p

piano

What other words start with the letter p?

p _____   p _____

p _____   p _____

Q q

queen

What other words start with the letter q?

q   q

q   q

R r

robot

What other words start with the letter r?

r

r

r

r

S s

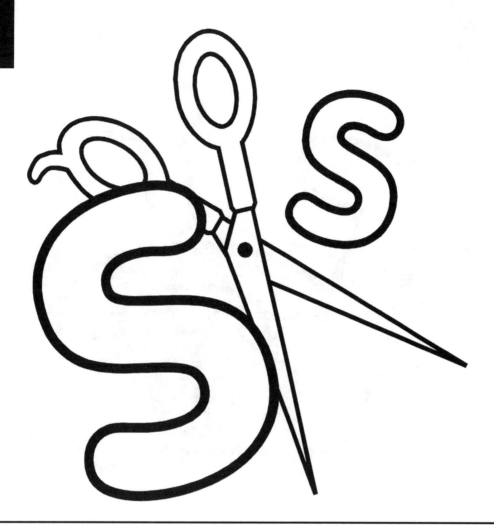

scissors

What other words start with the letter s?

s   s

s   s

T t

telephone

What other words start with the letter t?

U u

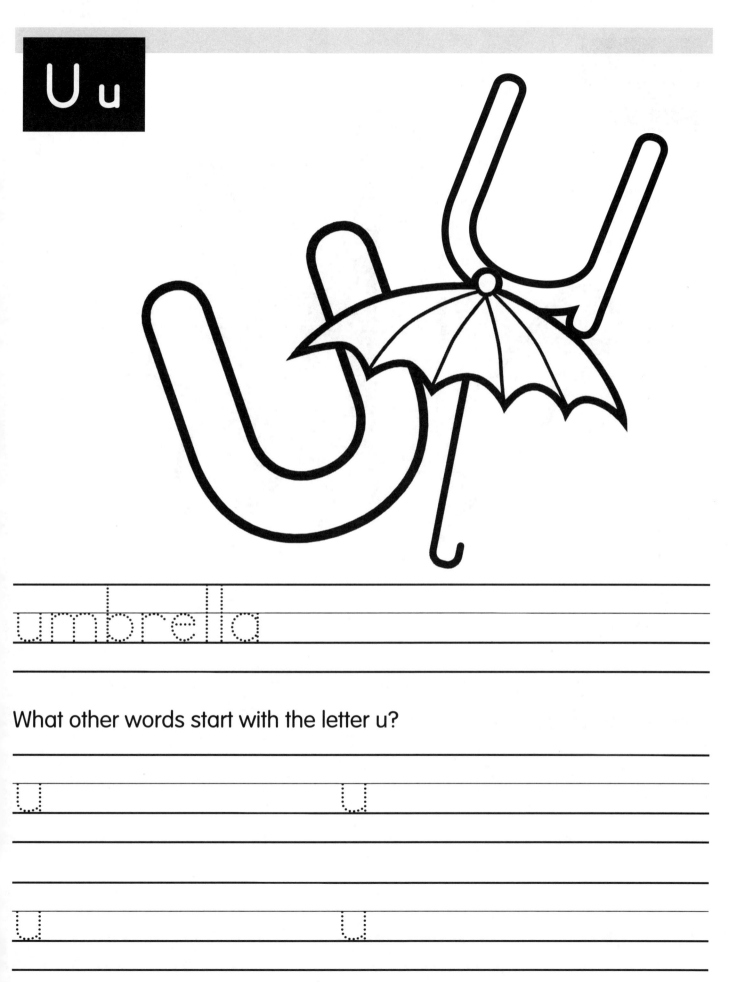

umbrella

What other words start with the letter u?

u   u

u   u

V v

violin

What other words start with the letter v?

V   v

V   v

W w

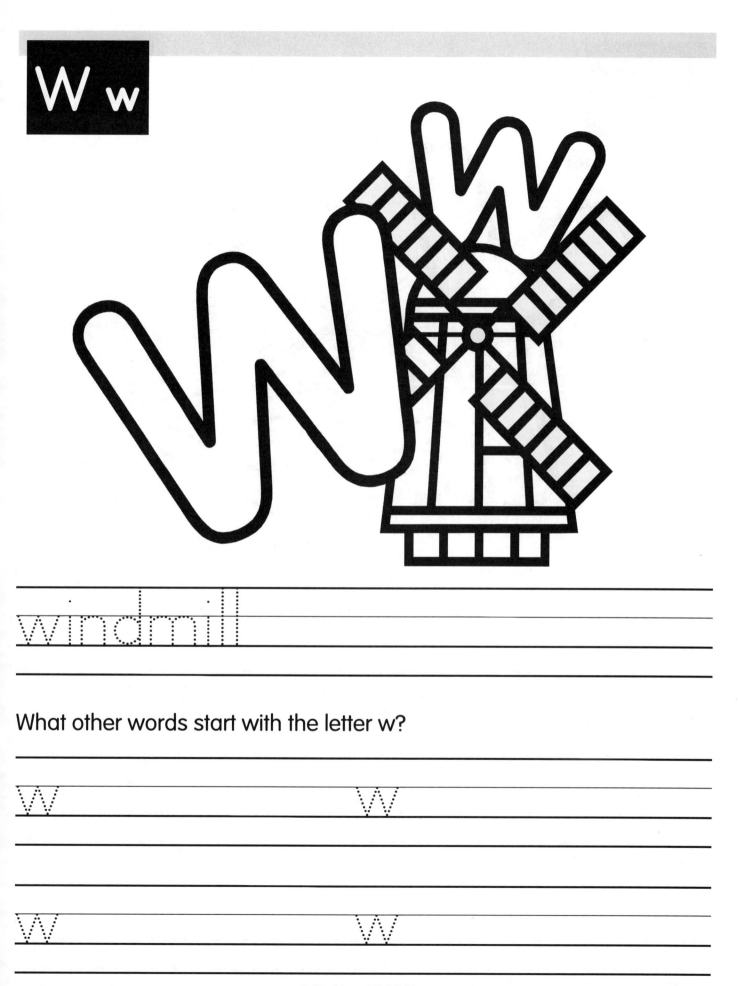

windmill

What other words start with the letter w?

w   w

w   w

xylophone

What other words start with the letter x?

X   X

X   X

Y y

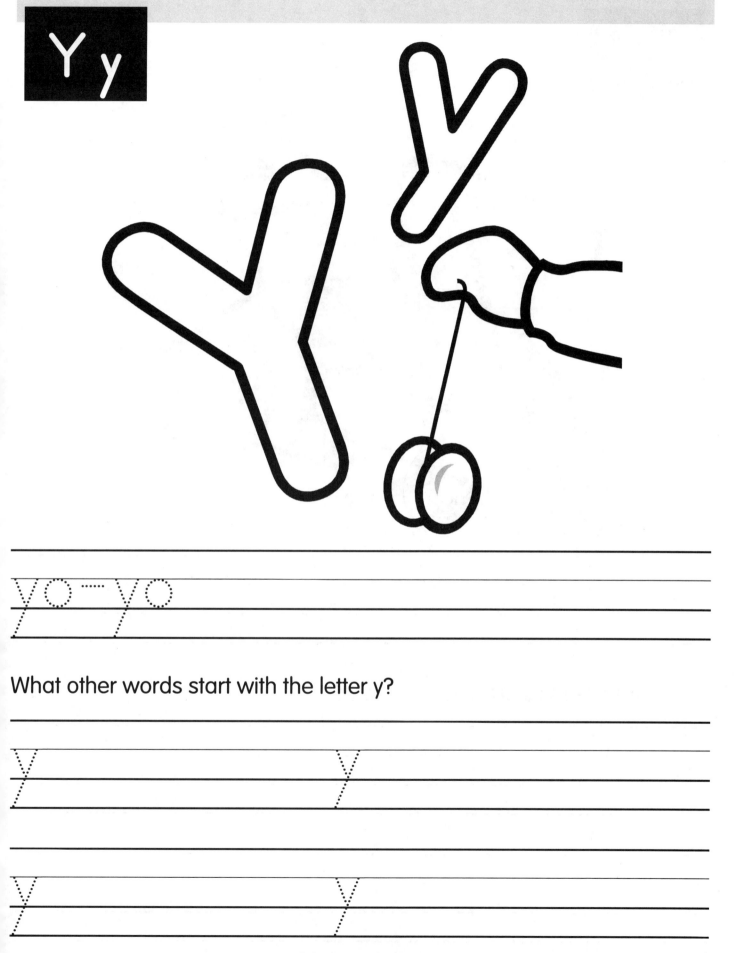

yo-yo

What other words start with the letter y?

y .... y

y .... y

Z z

zebra

What other words start with the letter z?

Z   Z

Z   Z

More Printing Practice – Provinces and Territories

Alberta

British Columbia

Manitoba

New Brunswick

Newfoundland and Labrador

Northwest Territories

Nunavut

Nova Scotia

Ontario

Prince Edward Island

Québec

Saskatchewan

Yukon

Brandon

Calgary

Charlottetown

Edmonton

Iqaluit

Moncton

Montréal

Ottawa

Québec

Regina

Saint John

Saskatoon

St. John's

Summerside

Toronto

More Printing Practice – Cities (continued)

Vancouver

Victoria

Whitehorse

Winnipeg

Yellowknife

More Printing Practice

What province do you live in?

_____
_____
_____

What city do you live in?

_____
_____
_____

What street do you live on?

_____
_____
_____

What is your favourite animal?

_____
_____
_____

What is your favourite food?

_____
_____
_____

Where is your favourite place to play?

_____
_____
_____

1

1

2

2

3

3

4

4

5

5

6

6

7

7

8

8

9

9

0

0

What is your phone number?

What is the year?   How many people in your family?

How old is your best friend?   Print your favourite numbers.

Printing Practice — Colours

Fill the spots with the correct colour. Trace and print the colour name.

yellow

blue

red

orange

green

purple

brown

Printing Practice — Days of the Week

Trace and print the days of the week.

Monday

Tuesday

Wednesday

Thursday

Friday

Saturday

Sunday

Trace and print the following months of the year. Colour the pictures.

January

February

March

April

May

June

© Chalkboard Publishing

Trace and print the following months of the year. Colour the pictures.

July

August

September

October

November

December

Printing Practice - Seasons of the Year

Trace and print the following seasons of the year. Colour the pictures.

spring   summer

autumn   winter

Animal Printing Fun!

cat

ant

dog

pig

bird

bat

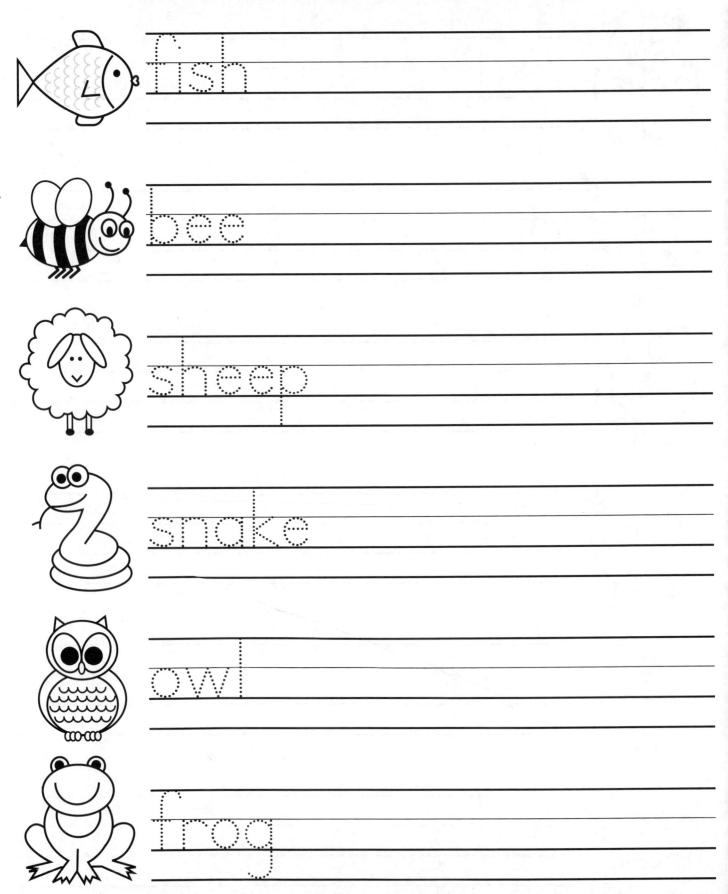

fish

bee

sheep

snake

owl

frog

Food Printing Fun!

 apple

 carrot

 broccoli

 potato

 lemon

 banana

pear

eggplant

cucumber

garlic

onion

orange

Title: _____

_____

_____

_____

_____

_____

_____

_____

_____

Title: _____

_____
_____
_____
_____

_____
_____

_____
_____

_____
_____

Title: _____

_____
_____
_____
_____
_____
_____
_____
_____
_____
_____

Title: _____

Title: _____

_____
_____
_____
_____
_____
_____
_____
_____
_____
_____

Title: _____

_____

_____

_____

_____

_____

_____

_____

_____

_____

_____

Printing Rubric

Name _____ Date _____

	Emergent	Developing	Capable	Mastered
Letter Shape	Few letters are formed correctly.	Some letters are formed correctly.	Most of the letters are formed correctly.	Almost all letters are formed correctly.
Slant of Letters	Little uniformity in slant of letters.	Some uniformity in slant of letters.	Good uniformity in slant of letters.	Excellent uniformity in slant of letters.
Connection to the Line	Few letters are within the lines.	Some letters are within the lines.	Most letters are within the lines.	Almost all letters are within the lines.
Letter Spacing	Few letters are spaced appropriately.	Some letters are spaced appropriately.	Most letters are spaced appropriately.	Almost all letters are spaced appropriately.
Neatness	Few letters/ words are legible.	Some letters/ words are legible.	Most letters/ words are legible.	Almost all letters/ words are legible.
Daily Work	Printing skills learned are rarely applied to daily work.	Printing skills learned are sometimes applied to daily work.	Printing skills learned are usually applied to daily work.	Printing skills learned are consistently applied to daily work.

Observations:

_____

_____

_____

Letters Requiring Practice:

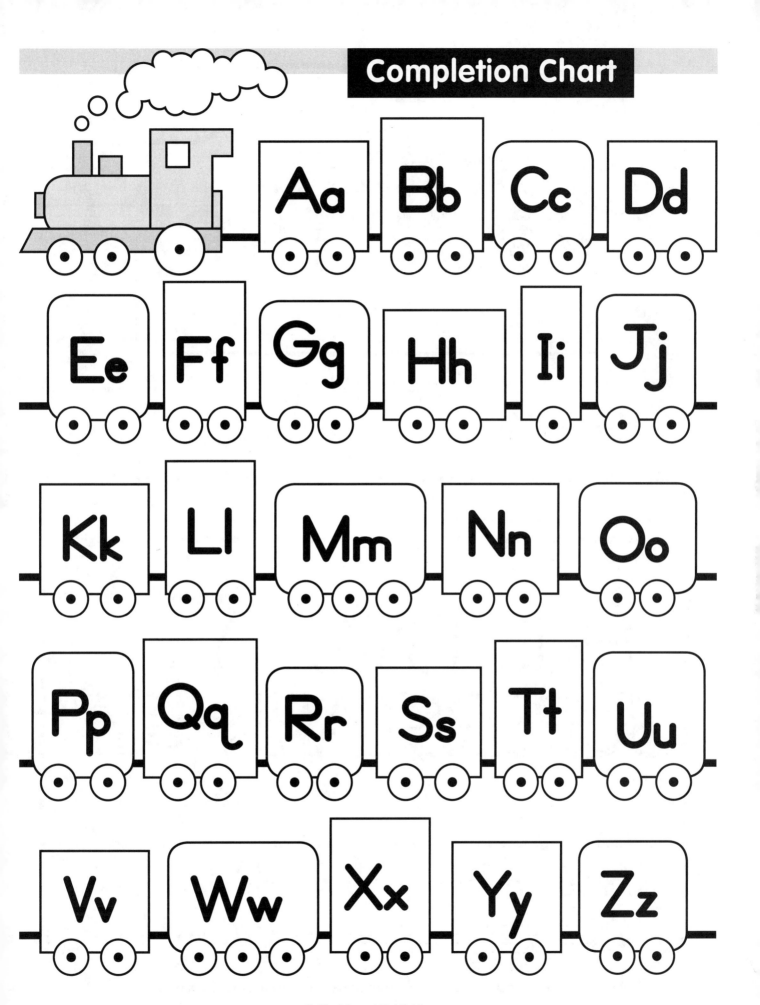

GREAT PRINTING!

_____

Keep it up!

PRINTING SUPERSTAR!

_____

Keep up the good work!